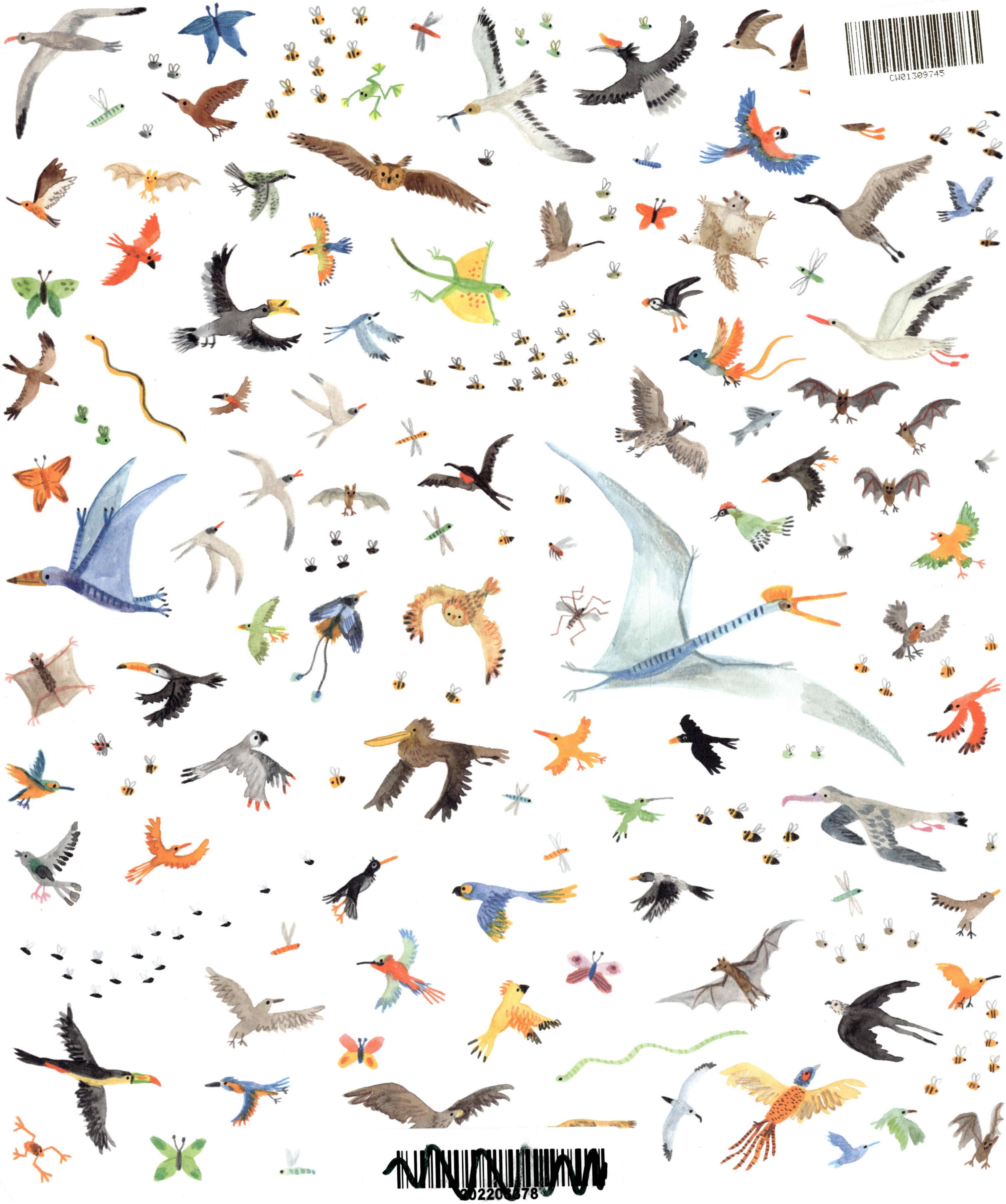

For Mya Rose Craig and all young people who fight
to protect our beautiful planet – N.D.
For Tom, for reminding me to always look up! – L.S.

HODDER CHILDREN'S BOOKS
First published in Great Britain in 2022 by Hodder and Stoughton

Text copyright © Nicola Davies, 2022
Illustrations copyright © Lorna Scobie, 2022

The moral rights of the author and illustrator have been asserted.
All rights reserved

A CIP catalogue record for this book is available from the British Library.

ISBN: 978 1 444 94842 4

1 3 5 7 9 10 8 6 4 2

Printed and bound in China

Hodder Children's Books
An imprint of Hachette Children's Group
Part of Hodder and Stoughton
Carmelite House
50 Victoria Embankment
London, EC4Y 0DZ

An Hachette UK Company
www.hachette.co.uk
www.hachettechildrens.co.uk

The MAGIC of FLIGHT

Nicola Davies and Lorna Scobie

Hodder Children's Books

INTRODUCTION

WHO HASN'T DREAMED OF BEING ABLE TO FLY?

For many animals, flight is not a dream but an everyday reality and an essential part of their survival kit. Even a short glide can mean the difference between life and death, offering a quick escape from predators.

But the ability to really fly — to get into the air, stay there and choose a direction — opens up all sorts of possibilities. Flying animals can travel through the air ten times faster than animals of the same size can run on land. This means that even the tiniest fliers can search further for food, mates and places to live than non-flying creatures.

However, flying isn't easy. Finding the balance between body weight, wing size and muscle strength is a puzzle that evolution has solved in different ways, giving us flying creatures as diverse as mosquitoes and albatrosses.

The creatures that have mastered flight have become some of the most successful on Earth. Their relationships with plants, as pollinators and seed spreaders, make them vital to the health of habitats everywhere, and to our food crops.

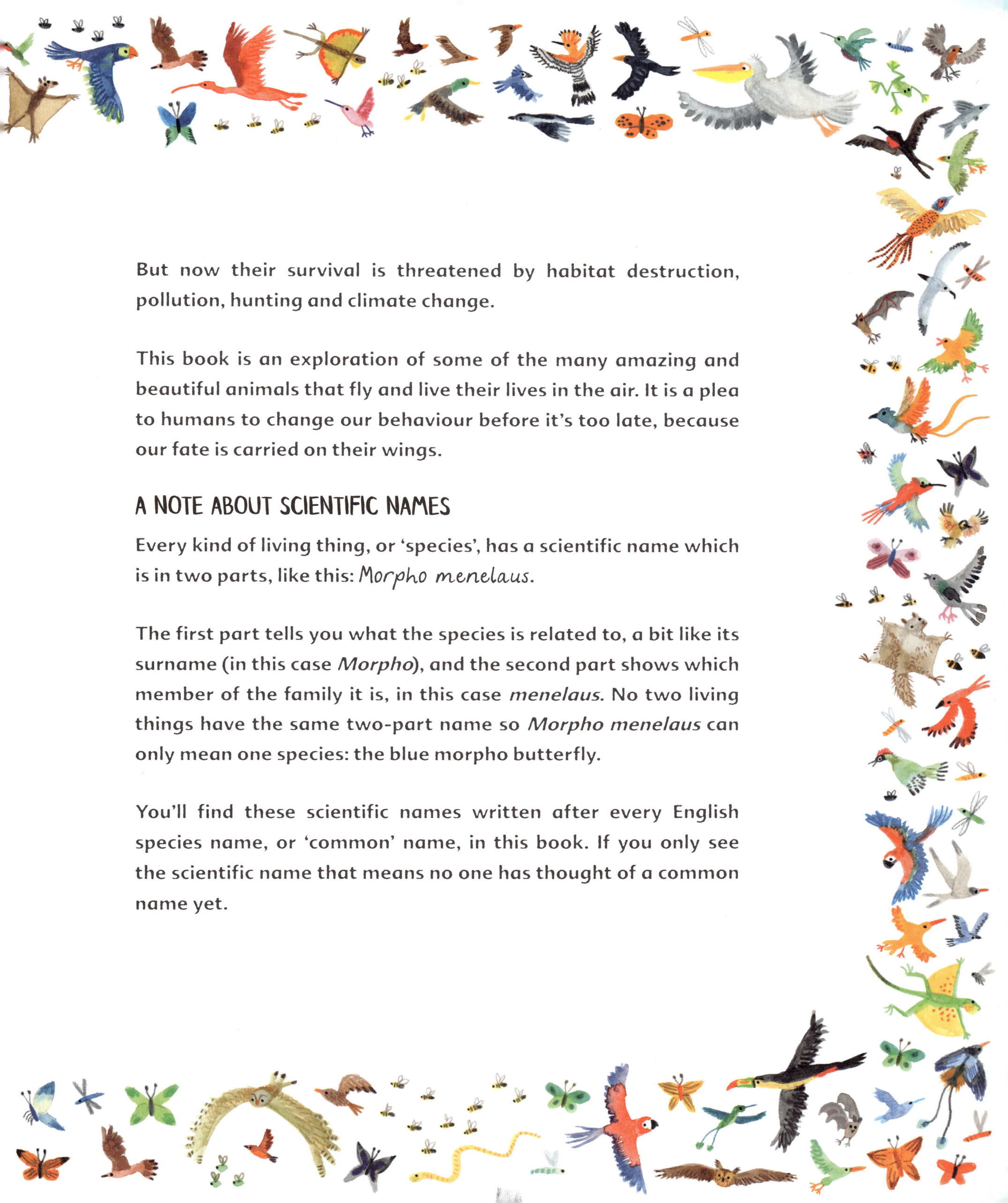

But now their survival is threatened by habitat destruction, pollution, hunting and climate change.

This book is an exploration of some of the many amazing and beautiful animals that fly and live their lives in the air. It is a plea to humans to change our behaviour before it's too late, because our fate is carried on their wings.

A NOTE ABOUT SCIENTIFIC NAMES

Every kind of living thing, or 'species', has a scientific name which is in two parts, like this: *Morpho menelaus*.

The first part tells you what the species is related to, a bit like its surname (in this case *Morpho*), and the second part shows which member of the family it is, in this case *menelaus*. No two living things have the same two-part name so *Morpho menelaus* can only mean one species: the blue morpho butterfly.

You'll find these scientific names written after every English species name, or 'common' name, in this book. If you only see the scientific name that means no one has thought of a common name yet.

GLIDING AND SOARING

Gliding is the simplest way to get airborne. Animals can glide by dropping from a height or by picking up speed and leaping into the air. Gliding animals can't stay airborne, as they lack the ability to flap, so their flights lose height fast and can't last long. But even a short glide can be useful!

Gliding from tree to tree

Climbing trees and crossing the forest floor is tiring and dangerous for small animals. Gliding uses less energy and is a handy way to escape quickly from predators.

SUGAR GLIDERS glide on skin stretched between their front and back legs.

DRACO LIZARDS have ribs that fan out with skin stretched between them.

SUGAR GLIDER
(Petaurus breviceps)

SUNDA COLUGO
(Galeopterus variegatus)

SULAWESI LINED GLIDING LIZARD
(Draco spilonotus)

COLUGOS can glide from tree to tree using a flap of furred skin stretched between their fingers and their front and hind legs.

WALLACE'S FLYING FROG
(Rhacophorus nigropalmatus)

Extra-big webbed feet help **FLYING FROGS** to glide a little so they can jump even further.

PARADISE TREE SNAKE
(Chrysopelea paradisi)

Even some tree snakes get in on the gliding act. **FLYING SNAKES** can flatten their bodies and curve their undersides to turn a fall into a glide that carries them to the next tree.

SAILFIN FLYING FISH
(Parexocoetus brachypterus)

MONEY SPIDER
(Erigone atra)

EUROPEAN HONEY BUZZARD
(Pernis apivorus)

Gliding fish

So-called **FLYING FISH** escape from underwater predators by picking up speed then shooting through the surface and spreading their large fins in the air. They can glide for up to 400m before they have to plop back into the water.

Electric ballooning

When baby spiders are ready to leave home, they release a fan of silken threads into the air. The silk has a small electrical charge, which reacts with the natural electrical field of the air, pulling the silk and the tiny spider up and away.

No need to flap

Many animals that are capable of powered flight often fly without flapping their wings. They may use rising air currents, called 'thermals', to lift them up – this is called soaring – or they may glide to take off from a height or to save energy while flying.

FIRST TRUE FLIGHTS

In Earth's long history just four groups of animals have evolved powered flight. This ability was so much more useful than gliding that each of these groups became very successful and evolved a huge variety of flying species.

First to fly: Insects

Fossils show that many flying insects existed 318 million years ago, and for 150 million years insects were the only flying creatures on Earth. Most modern insects can fly, and they are very successful as a result, making up more than half of all animal species.

Some of the first flying insects were **GRIFFINFLIES**. These were similar to modern dragonflies, but much bigger, with wingspans up to 70cm.

GRIFFINFLY

MODERN DRAGONFLIES

Nemicolopterus crypticus

Second up: Reptiles

Next into the air, 220 million years ago, were the **PTEROSAURS**, a group of reptiles that shared the Earth with the dinosaurs. This group included both the largest creatures ever to fly, as well as small species, like the blackbird-sized **NEMICOLOPTERUS**.

Archaeornithura meemannae

PTEROSAUR

Third place: Birds

ARCHAEOPTERYX, a pigeon-sized animal that lived 150 million years ago, is often called 'the first bird', but it couldn't fly as well as modern birds and had many of the features of the theropod dinosaurs from which it evolved. One of the first true birds was the little sparrow-sized ARCHAEORNITHURA MEEMANNAE that lived over 130 million years ago. From there, birds really took off, and today there are more species of birds than there are of reptiles, amphibians or mammals.

Last but not least

The oldest bat fossils show that bats very similar to the ones we know today were flying about 50 million years ago. Now there are over a thousand different species of bat – more than any other mammal group except rodents.

Onychonycteris finneyi

BAT FOSSIL

MYSTERY HISTORY

We know that flying animals evolved from animals that couldn't fly. But how did that happen? Were the first wings small and perhaps used for something other than flying? Did flight begin by gliding, or by running or jumping? Scientists can gather clues from fossils and from animals living today.

MAYFLY LARVAE

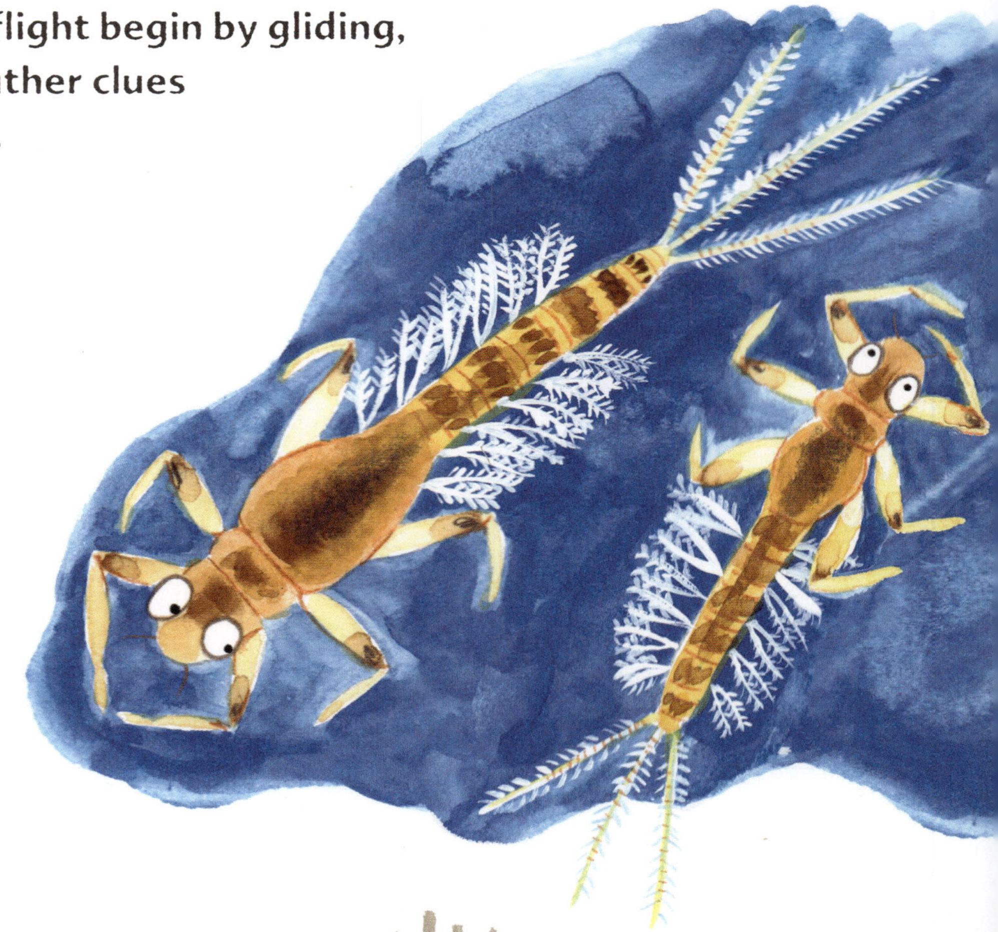

In water or on land?

Fossils show that there were many kinds of flying insects 318 million years ago. So insect wings must have evolved much earlier, perhaps from little flaps of exoskeleton that helped with camouflage or communication, or perhaps from the flapping gills of insects living in water, like the larvae of the mayfly.

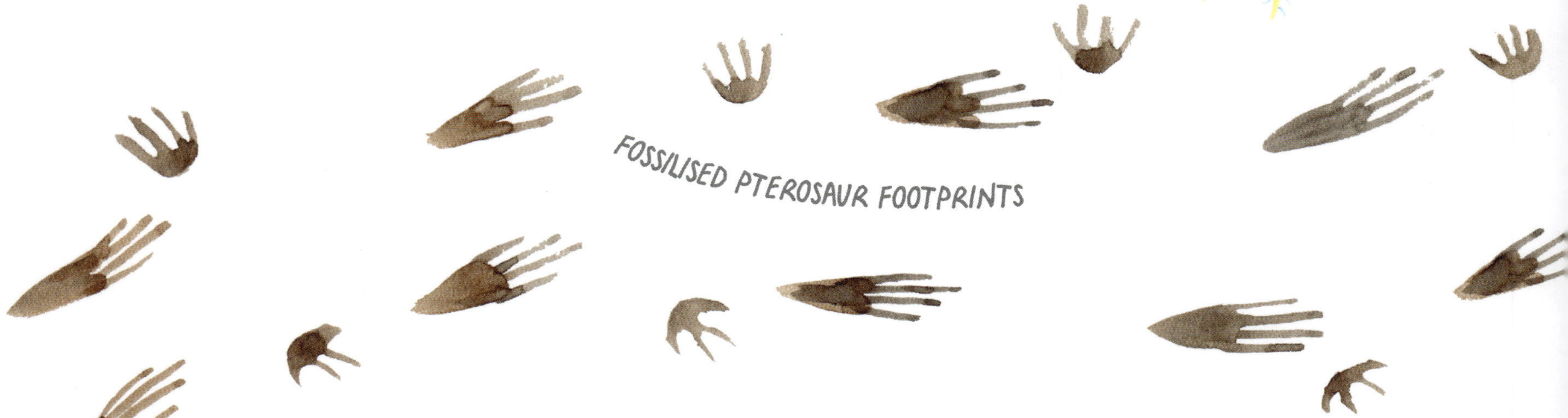

FOSSILISED PTEROSAUR FOOTPRINTS

Tracks show the way

Fossilised pterosaur footprints show that they used their winged front limbs as well as their back legs when walking, just as some bats do. Some bats can jump straight off the ground to take off, and pterosaurs did the same. But bats usually prefer to drop from a height and glide, so scientists think that this is how they, and pterosaurs, evolved the ability to fly.

The most famous fossil

ARCHAEOPTERYX was discovered in 1861 and became world famous because it had bird-like wings and feathers, but a long, bony tail and teeth like a reptile. It was named a 'missing link', as it showed that birds had evolved from theropod dinosaurs that walked on their back legs, leaving their front legs free to become wings.

How did Archaeopteryx fly?

The answer is . . . not very well! Archaeopteryx had rounded wings with symmetrical flight feathers and lacked big, powerful flight muscles, so it would have been a rather clumsy flier.

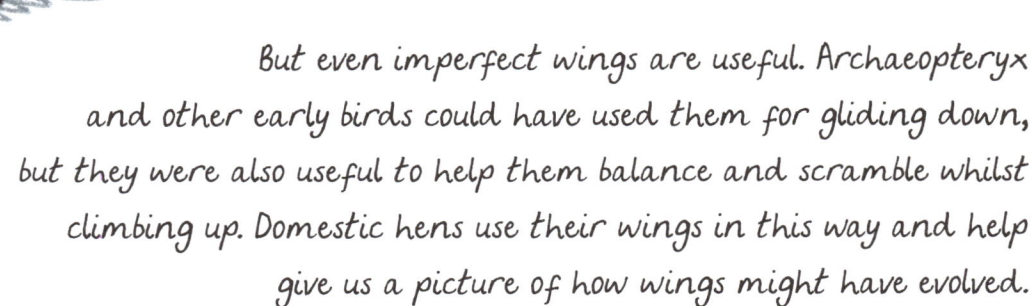

ARCHAEOPTERYX FOSSIL

Archaeopteryx lithographica

But even imperfect wings are useful. Archaeopteryx and other early birds could have used them for gliding down, but they were also useful to help them balance and scramble whilst climbing up. Domestic hens use their wings in this way and help give us a picture of how wings might have evolved.

Feathers before flight

Fossils have shown that many dinosaurs had feathers that were coloured and patterned just like birds' feathers today. This shows that feathers evolved for warmth, shade, display and camouflage. Using them for flight came later.

Tianyulong confuciusi

FLYING RECORDS

Biggest

QUETZALCOATLUS
A pterosaur that lived 65 million years ago
Wingspan: 11m

Smallest

FAIRY FLY
(Kikiki Huna)
A type of wasp measuring just 0.15mm long
Wingspan: 0.3mm

BEE HUMMINGBIRD
(Mellisuga helenae)
The smallest bird, weighing just 2g
Wingspan: 3cm

Fastest

PEREGRINE FALCON
(Falco peregrinus)
Up to **299kph** when diving on prey

Fastest wingbeat

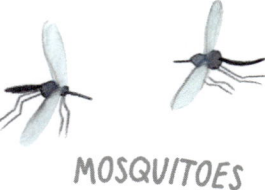

MOSQUITOES
(Anopheles funestus)
Can beat their wings over **1,000 times** a second

MALE RUBY-THROATED HUMMINGBIRD
(Archilochus colubris)
Shows off to females with **200 wingbeats** a second

Highest

RÜPPELL'S GRIFFON VULTURE
(Gyps rueppellii)
Soars up to **11,278m**

Longest flight

BAR-TAILED GODWIT
(Limosa lapponica)

A **BAR-TAILED GODWIT** made the longest recorded non-stop flight of **12,000km** between Alaska and New Zealand.

Furthest

PAINTED LADY BUTTERFLIES
(Vanessa cardui)
Fly **14,000km** from Africa to the Arctic

ARCTIC TERNS
(Sterna paradisaea)
Fly from the Arctic to the Antarctic and back, covering **96,000km**

Most numerous

RED-BILLED QUELEA
(Quelea quelea)
The most numerous birds on Earth. They can gather in a flock of a billion!

VERTEBRATE WINGS

All wings have evolved to do the same job. This is why wings of different animals, although made in different ways, look quite similar.

LIFT AND DRAG

All wings are an 'aerofoil' shape, curved on the top and flat on the bottom. This shape directs the air flowing underneath downwards, creating an upward force on the wing which generates **LIFT**. This is what keeps flying animals in the air.

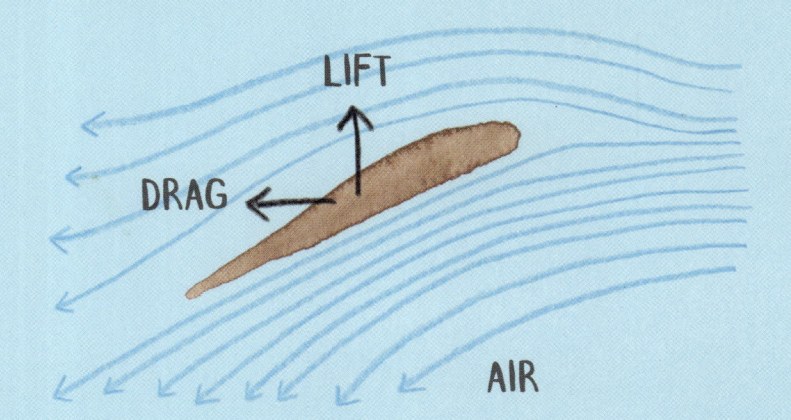

But the faster a wing moves, the more the air catches on it and pulls it back. This is called **DRAG**. Wings are shaped to try and maximise lift and minimise drag!

LIFT
DRAG
AIR

Wing bones

The wings of **PTEROSAURS**, **BIRDS** and **BATS** are supported by similar bones to those in your arm and hand. But the way that the bones are arranged in each group is different, because each group evolved the ability to fly separately.

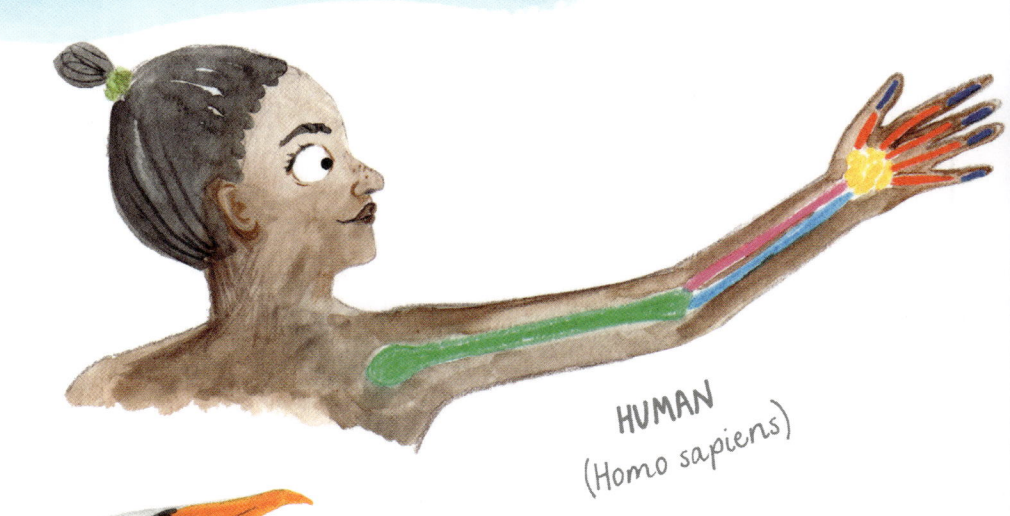

HUMAN
(Homo sapiens)

COMMON PIPISTRELLE BAT
(Pipistrellus pipistrellus)

NAZCA BOOBY
(Sula granti)

[Labels on bat illustration:]
THUMB, WRIST, INDEX FINGER, MIDDLE FINGER, RING FINGER, LITTLE FINGER, ELBOW, SHOULDER, ANKLE

HONDURAN WHITE BAT (Ectophylla alba)

Super flexible bat wings

BAT wings have four long fingers with skin stretched between them and the ankle. There are 20 different flexible joints in the wings, controlled by five sets of muscles. So bats can change the shape, surface area and curve of their wings, making them the most manoeuvrable of all fliers.

PTEROSAUR

Feathers

Flight feathers in birds' wings are strong and stiff. When they wear out they are replaced, so wings are always in top condition. Birds can bend or straighten their wings and separate their flight feathers, but compared with bat wings, bird wings are rather inflexible!

Naked or furry?

Pterosaur wings were made of skin stretched between one long finger and the back legs. The skin was stiffened by fibres and in some cases covered in a feather-like down for warmth.

INSECT WINGS

Insects are invertebrates, with a tough exoskeleton like a suit of armour, made of a material called chitin. Their wings are transparent sheets made of chitin, criss-crossed with tubes called veins, which help keep wings strong and nourished with food and oxygen.

HOUSEFLY
(Musca domestica)

BLUE DASHER DRAGONFLY
(Pachydiplax longipennis)

Two or four

Most insects have two pairs of wings which beat together in time. Only **DRAGONFLIES** beat their two pairs separately, whilst **TRUE FLIES** have just one pair of wings. Their second pair have evolved to become tiny movement sensors called 'halteres'.

WESTERN HONEY BEE
(Apis mellifera)

Hooked up

Many insects have a row of hooks on the hind wings to keep them joined to the front wings.

EUROPEAN EARWIG
(Forficula auricularia)

elytra

Wing origami

The front wings of **BEETLES** and **EARWIGS** have become tough shields called 'elytra', which cover the folded hind wings when they aren't in use. Earwig wings fold to a tenth of their size and can unfold and lock open ready for flight.

Efficient flappers

Insects have clever ways to get the most out of every flap; they beat their wings in a figure of eight to get lift on the upstroke as well as the down, and create swirls of air that give them an extra boost.

EUROPEAN HORNET
(Vespa crabro)

Scaly wings

BUTTERFLY and MOTH wings are covered with microscopic tile-like scales. These give the wings colour, but also help the insects slither out of spiders' webs or predators' mouths, leaving just their dusty scales behind.

MONARCH BUTTERFLY
(Danaus plexippus)

Flutter by, butterfly

Butterflies have wobbly flight, but this makes their movement unpredictable, making them harder to catch. They can still fly a long way; MONARCH BUTTERFLIES migrate from Canada to their winter home in Mexico.

VERTEBRATE POWER

Flying animals have some of the most powerful and hard-working muscles in nature, so they need efficient ways to deliver oxygen and energy to the flight muscles where it is most needed.

Chest power

Birds have a huge breastbone, called the keel, which anchors the big muscles that move the wing. These muscles work by pulling on tendons attached to wing bones.

Bats need to be small enough to crawl into crevices to roost, so they don't have a big keel. Instead, they move their wings using several sets of muscles in their chest and back.

upstroke

downstroke

MOUNTAIN BLACKEYE
(Zosterops emiliae)

Blood and air

Birds have hearts that are ten times bigger for their size than ours. Their lungs are connected to air sacs in their bodies and bones, and air flows just one way around this system. This means that birds get more oxygen out of each breath and can deliver it to the muscles faster. Hard-working flight muscles make a lot of heat and air sacs also help to keep birds cool as they fly.

EURASIAN GOLDEN ORIOLE
(Oriolus oriolus)

Power saver

Bats' hearts are larger for their size than other mammals', and their lungs are super efficient. This keeps their flight muscles supplied with oxygen and fuel carried in their blood. They can change the shape of their wings more than birds can, reducing the effort needed to flap them and making them more manoeuvrable.

HUMAN BONE

BAT BONE

PTEROSAUR BONE

BIRD BONE

Keeping it light

Birds, bats and pterosaurs evolved lightweight skeletons to help them get airborne. Bats' wing bones are very thin and delicate and birds' bones are full of holes, like honeycomb. But the masters of light bones were the pterosaurs whose bones were hollow tubes.

Flight feedback

Like an airline pilot reading her instruments, all flying animals use their senses to monitor air currents, height and speed to keep their flight safe and efficient.

INSECT POWER

Nothing can match the manoeuvrability of an insect in flight. They can hover, fly backwards and even upside down — turning many times in a fraction of a second.

Muscles in a box

Insects have chests like little boxes, with muscles on the inside. These work in one of two way.

In some insects, such as **DRAGONFLIES**, muscles poke through the box and pull directly on the ends of the wings to raise and lower them.

In most insects, one set of muscles pulls the top of the chest down, making the wings pop up. The other set pulls on the front and the back of the box, pushing the wings down.

Small and speedy

Most insects beat their wings very fast, between 50 and 1,000 wingbeats per second. Their muscles can work more quickly and efficiently than the muscles of any other group of animals.

muscles

EMPEROR DRAGONFLY
(Anax imperator)

HOUSEFLY
(Musca domestica)

muscles

BROWN HEATH ROBBERFLY
(Machimus cingulatus)

EUROPEAN WASP
(Vespula germanica)

MEADOW GRASSHOPPER
(Pseudochorthippus parallelus)

air sacs

spiracles

COMMON FRUIT FLY
(Drosophila melanogaster)

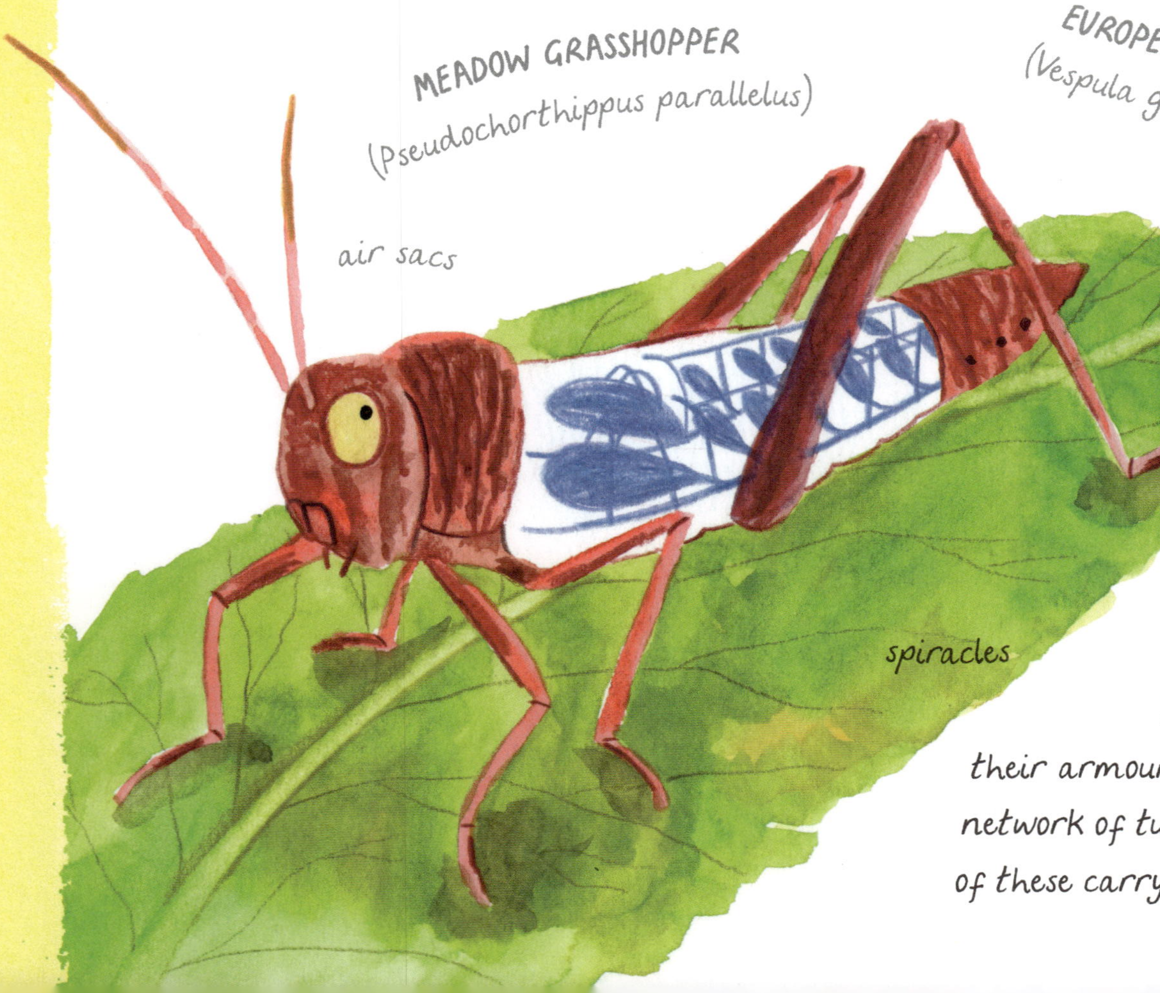

Air in microtubes

Insects breathe through tiny holes in their armour-like skin called 'spiracles', which connect with a network of tubes and sacs throughout their bodies. The smallest of these carry oxygen to microscopic parts of the flight muscles.

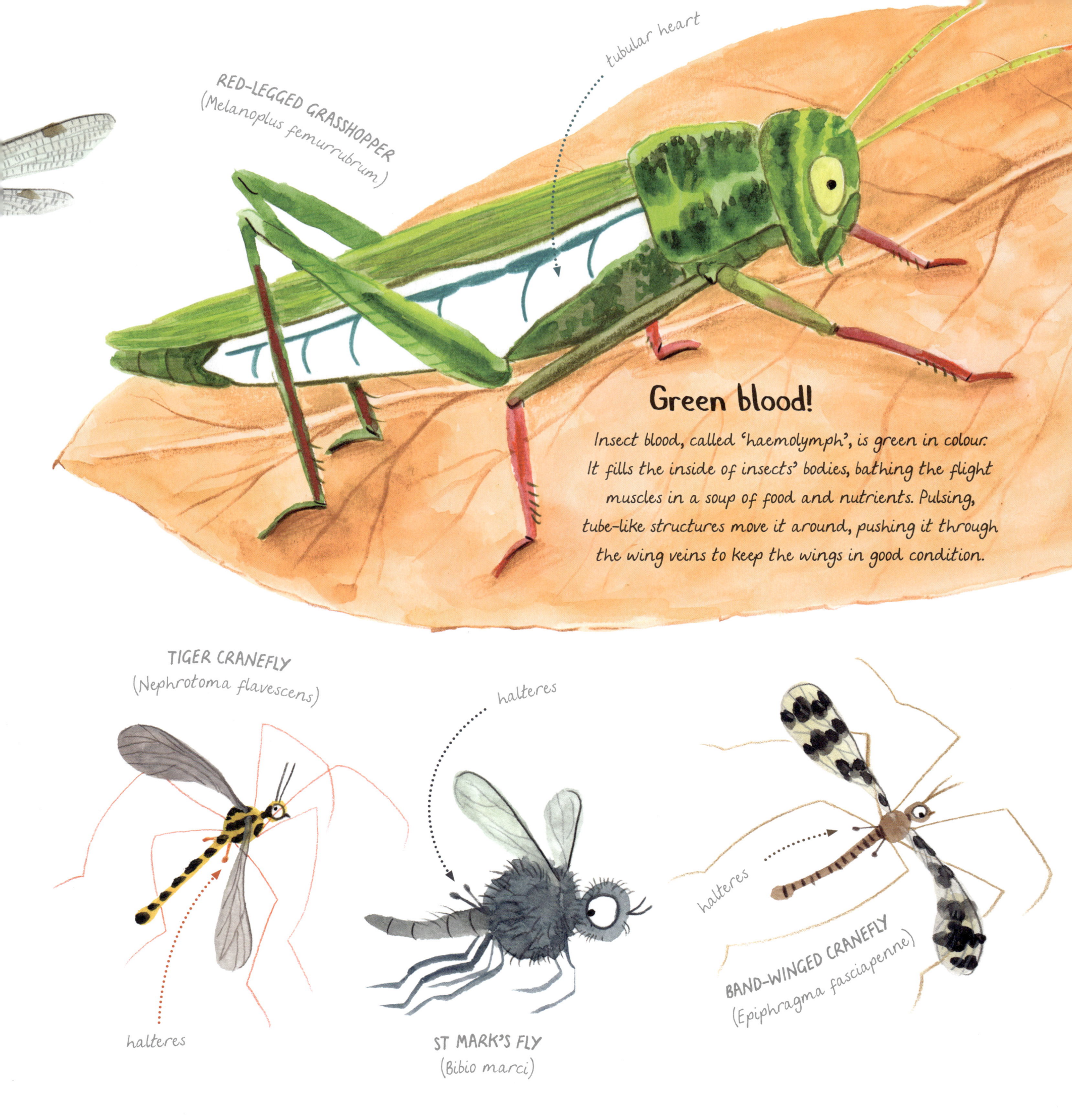

RED-LEGGED GRASSHOPPER
(Melanoplus femurrubrum)

tubular heart

Green blood!

Insect blood, called 'haemolymph', is green in colour. It fills the inside of insects' bodies, bathing the flight muscles in a soup of food and nutrients. Pulsing, tube-like structures move it around, pushing it through the wing veins to keep the wings in good condition.

TIGER CRANEFLY
(Nephrotoma flavescens)

halteres

ST MARK'S FLY
(Bibio marci)

halteres

BAND-WINGED CRANEFLY
(Epiphragma fasciapenne)

halteres

Micro monitoring

Insects' high-speed manoeuvres depend on detailed feedback about how each wing is moving every fraction of a second. In **TRUE FLIES** some of this information comes from the halteres, which beat in time with the wings and are loaded with sensors.

CLEVER FEATHERS

Fossils show that many dinosaurs had small, fluffy feathers for warmth and colour. It took 100 million years for bigger, flatter feathers to evolve, so that the first birds could spread their wings and fly.

Flight and fit

Each wing has big flight feathers rooted in the bones, with smaller feathers filling in the gaps and covering the body for warmth. Each feather can be raised and lowered so birds can change the shape of their wings in flight, or fluff out their feathers to keep warm!

smooth feathers

fluffed out

GREAT HORNED OWL
(Bubo virginianus)

Feather care

Birds preen every day to keep their feathers in top condition. They run their flight feathers through their beaks to keep them smooth and clean. They rub oil from the preen gland on their tails over their feathers to keep them waterproof, and they may bathe in water or dust.

TREE SWALLOW
(Tachycineta bicolor)

ASIAN GREEN BEE-EATER
(Merops orientalis)

Flight ready

Feathers can't be mended, so at least once a year birds moult all their worn-out feathers and grow new ones. Most birds moult flight feathers symmetrically, one on each side at a time, so they can keep flying.

ORIENTAL PIED HORNBILL
(Anthracoceros albirostris)

RUFOUS FANTAIL
(Rhipidura rufifrons)

Tails too

Tail feathers are an important part of a bird's flying kit. They can be held together to point or spread like a fan to give the bird extra lift and to help with steering and landing.

NEW ZEALAND FANTAIL
(Rhipidura fuliginosa)

BALD EAGLE SKELETON

BALD EAGLE
(Haliaeetus leucocephalus)

How many feathers?

Most birds have around 25 flight feathers in each wing, but the total number of body feathers depends on size – hummingbirds have 940 while swans have 25,000! Feathers can weigh more than a bird's skeleton; a **BALD EAGLE** has 272g of bone but 677g of feathers.

SHAPED FOR THE JOB

There are many kinds of flying creature, and their different lifestyles need different kinds of flight — and different kinds of wings!

PURPLE EMPEROR BUTTERFLY
(*Apatura iris*)

PRIVET HAWK-MOTH
(*Sphinx ligustri*)

Fluttering and zooming

BUTTERFLIES have broad wings, good for catching a breeze and fluttering slowly amongst branches. But **HAWK-MOTHS** have narrow wings and are some of the fastest of all insects.

HEN HARRIER
(*Circus cyaneus*)

SPARROWHAWK
(*Accipiter nisus*)

Short or long

SPARROWHAWKS hunt in woodland where long wings would get in the way, but **HEN HARRIERS** hunt out on open moorland where soaring matters more than the ability to duck and dive around trees.

Finger wings

VULTURES must fly far in search of food, so they need to use as little energy as possible. Long, broad wings catch 'thermals' — spirals of warm air rising off the ground — and each separate primary feather acts like a mini wing, supplying more low-cost lift.

BLACK VULTURE
(*Coragyps atratus*)

Ocean voyages

Narrow, pointed wings enable seabirds like **LAYSAN ALBATROSS** to ride air currents rising from the waves, and to use strong winds to glide effortlessly for long distances. But it's easier to take off from the water's surface with a bit of wind, so these birds thrive in rough weather.

LAYSAN ALBATROSS
(Phoebastria immutabilis)

Nectar feeding

HUMMINGBIRDS have short, pointed wings with a flexible shoulder joint. This allows them to move their wings in a figure of eight and flap them up to 200 times a second. They can hover in front of flowers to get nectar.

RUFOUS-TAILED HUMMINGBIRD
(Amazilia tzacatl)

HUMMINGBIRD HAWK-MOTHS also feed on nectar and have wings with a similar shape and flapping frequency to hummingbirds.

HUMMINGBIRD HAWK-MOTH
(Macroglossum stellatarum)

WHITE-THROATED SWIFT
(Aeronautes saxatalis)

Catching insects two ways

The skinny, pointed wings of **SWIFTS** are perfect for high-speed swoops and gulping insects high in the air. **SWALLOWS'** wings are broader — good for low-speed turning to grab fat bugs close to the ground.

BARN SWALLOW
(Hirundo rustica)

A RAINBOW OF WINGS

Wing shape and size are important for flight, but in birds, butterflies and moths, wing colours can also help in other ways — from camouflage to communication.

Hide out or say hello

Mottled browns give the **SCOPS OWL** camouflaged wings, good for hiding out in trees.

Birds such as the **HOOPOE** have feathers that fit together in bright bands of colour, so they can easily spot others of their kind.

The **INDIAN LEAFWING BUTTERFLY** has a camouflaged underside to its wing and a bright blue flash on top that says, 'here I am!'

EURASIAN SCOPS OWL
(Otus scops)

EURASIAN HOOPOE
(Upupa epops)

INDIAN LEAFWING BUTTERFLY
(Kallima paralekta)

NORTHERN GANNET
(Morus bassanus)

Dark strength

Most **GULLS** have white underwings so fish can't spot them against a bright sky. But the ends of their wings get the most wear and tear so they are black, full of the dark pigment 'melanin' that makes them stronger.

Mixing up a rainbow

Feathers and wing scales get their colours from pigments, like the dyes that colour clothes, and from microscopic layers that split light like a prism, called 'structural colours'. Combining pigments with structural colours results in an almost infinite palette.

The greens of **PARROTS** are created by a blue structural colour passing through a yellow pigment. Structural colours can make wings shine like jewels, like on the **MADAGASCAN SUNSET MOTH**.

GREAT GREEN MACAW
(Ara ambiguus)

Chrysozephyrus hisamatsusanus

MADAGASCAN SUNSET MOTH
(Chrysiridia rhipheus)

More than a rainbow

Unlike us, birds and insects can see ultraviolet light. The wings of the **CHRYSOZEPHYRUS HISAMATSUSANUS** look green to us, but gleam with ultraviolet light to butterfly eyes.

You wear what you eat

FLAMINGOS get their pink feathers from their diet of algae and shrimps!

WHITE-CHEEKED TURACOS get their unique green colour from their fruity diet.

WHITE-CHEEKED TURACO
(Menelikornis leucotis)

AMERICAN FLAMINGO
(Phoenicopterus ruber)

DEATH ON THE WING

Wings alone are not enough to make a successful airborne hunter — sharp eyes and deadly killing skills are essential too. Flying hunters can spot prey from a distance and ambush them from the sky.

Monkey grab

Large, forward-facing eyes give eagles sight that's eight times better than ours. Their strong feet can drive sharp talons into prey for a quick kill. The **PHILIPPINE EAGLE** is one of the largest, with a 2m wingspan, and can snatch flying lemurs, monkeys and fruit bats from the tops of rainforest trees.

PHILIPPINE EAGLE
(Pithecophaga jefferyi)

Dive master

Flying high above lakes and estuaries, **OSPREYS** can spot fish beneath the water and plunge down to grab them, sometimes going under the surface. Their nostrils have a valve to keep water out and their feet have spines for holding slippery fish.

OSPREY
(Pandion haliaetus)

PEREGRINE FALCON
(Falco peregrinus)

Stoop to kill

Deep-set eyes and dark feathers cut the sun's glare so **PEREGRINE FALCONS** can spot flying birds a mile away and thousands of metres below. They dive, or 'stoop', folding their wings to make an arrow shape, and hit their prey at speeds over 300kph, usually killing it instantly.

HOBBY
(Falco subbuteo)

Aerial pursuit

The **HOBBY** can keep fast-flying prey such as swifts or dragonflies in focus through many twists and turns. A quick grab with its legs and feet and it can eat its dinner on the wing.

GREEN DARNER DRAGONFLY
(Anax junius)

Deadlier than a lion

DRAGONFLIES have eyes that wrap round their heads, with colour vision ten times better than ours and brain cells specialised for tracking movement. This gives them a success rate of over 90% when they hunt. That's four times better than a lion.

Smallest assassins

ROBBER FLIES are as small as a grain of rice, but their huge eyes work like binoculars to spot flying prey, then keep it in focus for a fast pursuit and a final, accurate strike.

ROBBER FLY
(Holcocephala abdominalis)

GREAT ESCAPES

With each hunt a predator only stands to lose a meal, but their prey could lose their life. As hunters evolve better ways to hunt, their prey must evolve better ways to escape — so overall the odds are in favour of the hunted, not the hunter!

REDSHANK
(Tringa totanus)

Keeping a lookout

In flocks of birds there are many eyes on the lookout and the whole flock can be in the air less than half a second after one bird spots a threat.

Aerobatics

Before they roost, **STARLINGS** form huge flocks known as 'murmurations'. Together they perform incredible aerobatics to confuse flying predators.

Escaping by surprise

Birds like **GROUSE** and **PHEASANTS** leave flying until the last moment. Their chest muscles are made for explosive power, so they can shoot straight into the air, startling the predator and making a fast getaway.

COMMON PHEASANT
(Phasianus colchicus)

Bat vs moth

Moths have been trying to avoid being a bat's dinner for 50 million years and have evolved some clever escape tricks.

More than 50,000 species of moths have tiny drums of skin on their bodies which act like ears and are tuned to the high pitch of bat echolocation sounds. When a moth hears a bat, it folds its wings and dives to escape.

TIGER MOTHS, such as the RED-HEADED PYGARCTIA, can click to warn the bat that they are poisonous and not good to eat.

The GROTE'S BERTHOLDIA MOTH can even make sounds that copy bat sounds, scrambling the bat's echolocation so it gives up the chase.

Hunting bats go for a moth's body. The long tails on the hind wings of the LUNA MOTH make an echo like a body, confusing the bats into going for the tail and missing their target.

'eardrum'

LARGE YELLOW UNDERWING MOTH
(Noctua pronuba)

RED-HEADED PYGARCTIA MOTH
(Pygarctia roseicapitis)

GROTE'S BERTHOLDIA MOTH
(Bertholdia trigona)

LUNA MOTH
(Actias luna)

FLIGHT DISPLAYS

For flying animals, flight isn't just a way to get around in order to find food and shelter — it's a way of life. It plays a part in how they communicate, find a mate and chase off rivals.

Flying jewels

Male **HUMMINGBIRDS** show off their bright, shiny colours to impress females by hovering in front of them, jinking from side to side, and by diving straight down from high in the air. Some use their wings to make short buzzes of sound to add to the display.

COSTA'S HUMMINGBIRD
(Calypte costae)

Male **MARVELOUS SPATULETAILS** hover and wave their long spoon-shaped tail feathers.

Male **COSTA'S HUMMINGBIRDS** hover from side to side and spread their purple throat feathers.

MARVELOUS SPATULETAIL
(Loddigesia mirabilis)

COMMON BUZZARD
(Buteo buteo)

Airspace

Bird territories stretch up into the air. In spring, pairs of **BUZZARDS** will soar over their home, calling out and telling other buzzards that this is a no-fly zone for anyone but them!

Big feathers

Male **WIDOWBIRDS** have shiny black feathers and long tail plumes to help them stand out against the green grass when they fly straight up to impress females.

JACKSON'S WIDOWBIRD
(Euplectes jacksoni)

Scented wings

The pattern and colours of butterfly wings help them to find members of their own species. Once a male spots the right kind of female he'll fly up close, often releasing a scent from his wings that tells her he wants to mate with her.

Damsel and dragon courting

When male DAMSELFLIES and DRAGONFLIES spot a female they simply grab and hold onto her and the pair stays flying, forming a wheel shape in the air, as they mate.

COMMON BIRDWING BUTTERFLY
(Troides helena)

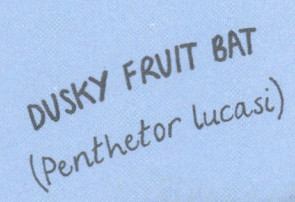

COMMON BLUE DAMSELFLY
(Enallagma cyathigerum)

DUSKY FRUIT BAT
(Penthetor lucasi)

Flight party

In late summer and autumn, some species of bats swarm at the entrance to their winter hibernation caves. As this is also mating season, scientists think that females could be using these flying parties to choose a mate.

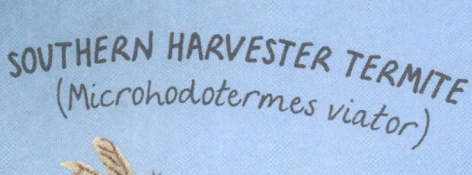

SOUTHERN HARVESTER TERMITE
(Microhodotermes viator)

Nuptial flights

Many ANTS, BEES and TERMITES live in big colonies, with one queen who lays all the eggs and thousands of workers doing everything else. In late summer, new queens hatch and fly into the air with a swarm of males who mate with them. Each queen will found a new colony of her own.

NIGHT FLIGHTS

The darkness of night is good cover for both predators and prey. But how have night fliers solved the problem of flying and finding food in the dark?

Owl solutions

From the tiny ELF OWL to the massive EAGLE-OWL, owls have solved the problems of night-time hunting.

Owl eyes are huge so they can see in the dimmest light. They are too big to move in their sockets, so owls have long necks that allow them to twist their heads to look around.

Hearing is the secret to owl success. The disc of feathers around an owl's face gathers sound for the ear holes, which are hidden under the feathers, one lower than the other. This allows owls to pinpoint sound, and prey, in three dimensions.

EURASIAN EAGLE-OWL
(Bubo bubo)

ELF OWL
(Micrathene whitneyi)

GREAT GREY OWL
(Strix nebulosa)

URAL OWL
(Strix uralensis)

Sharp ears that can locate prey are no good if your noisy flight gives you away! Owl feathers have a soft velvety surface so they can fly silently and pounce on unsuspecting prey.

Echolocation

BATS make high-pitched cries — higher than our ears can hear — then listen to their echoes to get a picture in sound so accurate that they can detect objects smaller than the width of a human hair. This incredible ability has made them the real rulers of the night, with more than 1,000 species in existence.

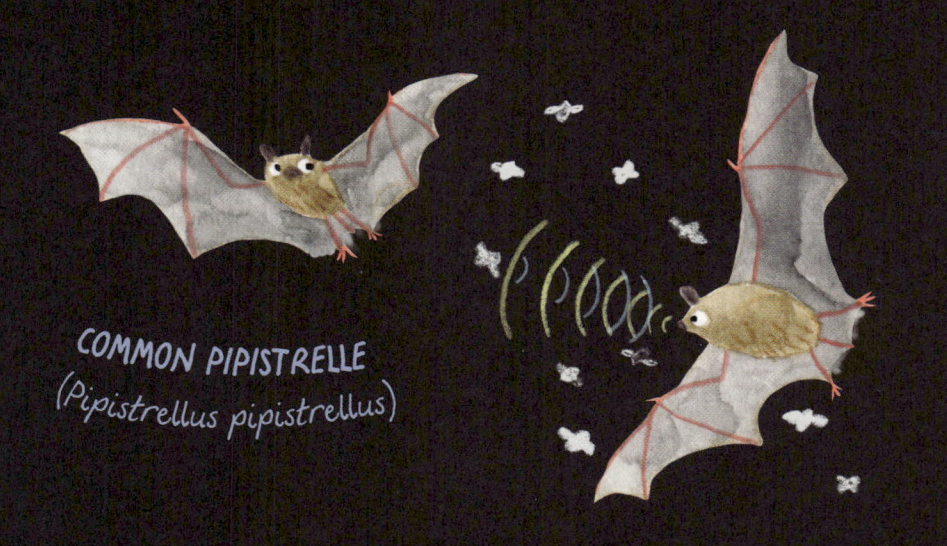

Many bats use echolocation to locate, chase and capture all sorts of night-flying insects. Tiny PIPISTRELLE BATS may catch 3,000 midges in one night, while PALLID BATS pounce on scorpions and are immune to their stings.

COMMON PIPISTRELLE
(Pipistrellus pipistrellus)

PALLID BAT
(Antrozous pallidus)

FISHERMAN BAT

FISHERMAN BATS echolocate ripples on the surface of ponds and grab fish with their large back feet.

SPECTRAL BATS use echolocation to hunt other bats and small mammals, which they then kill with a powerful bite. They have a 1m wingspan but weigh less than 200g so they can easily carry off heavy prey.

SPECTRAL BAT
(Vampyrum spectrum)

Louder than a rock band

High-pitched echolocation sounds don't travel very far, so bats need to shout very loud — as loud as a jet taking off. They avoid going deaf by disconnecting their own ears for the fraction of a second that each cry lasts.

OCEAN WANDERERS

The ocean is a rich source of food, but to make the most of it, flying animals must be able to endure waves, wind and storms. Only birds are tough enough, and more than 300 species are adapted for the demands of a life at sea.

WILSON'S STORM PETREL
(Oceanites oceanicus)

Dancing over the sea

STORM PETRELS are the tiniest of all seabirds, some weighing less than a tennis ball. They pick small fish, plankton and tiny squid from the sea's surface. They make easy prey for predators, so they return to their nests in clifftop burrows at night.

WANDERING ALBATROSS
(Diomedea exulans)

Wind riders

ALBATROSSES are found in the stormy Southern Ocean or the wild Pacific. They rely on strong winds so they can use their long wings to soar over the waves without needing to flap. They can cover 16,000km searching for squid to eat without returning to land.

COMMON GUILLEMOT
(Uria aalge)

Fly vs swim

Seabirds that dive to get their food need bodies that can fly and swim! **GUILLEMOTS** and **PUFFINS** have short wings that they have to flap fast, and they are poor at changing direction and landing. But their wings make excellent paddles underwater.

Pirates ahoy

FRIGATEBIRDS ride the spirals of warm air that rise off tropical oceans up to 4,000m, high in the clouds, and stay on the wing for weeks. They can't dive or rest on the sea as their feathers aren't waterproof, so they ambush birds in flight and steal their catch.

MAGNIFICENT FRIGATEBIRD
(Fregata magnificens)

CAPE GANNET
(Morus capensis)

Airbags

GANNETS dive from 40m to spear fish in the water, hitting the surface at over 80kph. Extensions of their breathing air sacs help to cushion the impact so they don't break to bits getting their dinner.

NORTHERN FULMAR
(Fulmarus glacialis)

Salt proof

Drinking sea water and eating sea creatures could load seabirds with too much salt. They cope by having a salt gland in their nostrils which pumps out super salty water that drips from their beaks. In some seabirds, like the **FULMAR**, the salt glands are in tubes on top of the beak. These birds are known as tubenoses.

A bellyful of fish

Many seabirds fly such long distances to find food that carrying it home for their chicks in their beaks isn't possible. Instead, they carry it in their stomachs and sick it up for their chicks when they get home.

ATLANTIC PUFFIN
(Fratercula arctica)

Long live seabirds!

Ocean life is hard work, so seabirds breed slowly, usually rearing just one or two chicks at a time. Many mate for life and live for a long time. **PUFFINS**, for example, can live for up to 33 years!

INCREDIBLE JOURNEYS

Every autumn, birds, butterflies and bats fly hundreds or even thousands of miles to escape winter weather, only returning in the spring. This mass migration of flying creatures is so enormous it shows up on radar screens! Four billion birds fly over the US alone every spring and autumn.

Migration mysteries

Modern technology is helping to uncover some of the mysterious details of migration journeys.

Until recently, no one knew where **PUFFINS** went in winter, but electronic tags have now tracked them far out at sea in the middle of the Atlantic.

ATLANTIC PUFFIN
(Fratercula arctica)

ARCTIC TERN
(Sterna paradisaea)

Bird ringing had already shown that **ARCTIC TERNS** fly from the Arctic to the Antarctic and back. But satellite tagging showed that some took the long way round and covered almost 100,000km in a year.

The **ANCIENT MURRELET** is a seabird that nests amongst tree roots in the forests of western Canada. When nesting is over, parents and young fly 8,000km east across the Pacific to waters that are just like the ones they left behind. No one knows why!

ANCIENT MURRELET
(Synthliboramphus antiquus)

Flight training

Before a long migration many birds pig out on the sweetest, fattiest foods they can find to fuel their journeys. Some can even increase the size of their hearts and the oxygen-carrying capacity of their blood.

MONARCH BUTTERFLY
(Danaus plexippus)

SEMIPALMATED SANDPIPER
(Calidris pusilla)

Tiny travellers

Every autumn, **MONARCH BUTTERFLIES** from the northeastern US and Canada fly up to 4,800km south to spend the winter in Mexico. When they fly north in spring, they go just far enough to lay eggs. Their children and grandchildren will complete the journey north by the end of the summer.

BARN SWALLOW
(Hirundo rustica)

BARNACLE GOOSE
(Branta leucopsis)

Stopovers

Some travellers can snack en route. **SWALLOWS** snap up insects as they travel. **BARNACLE GEESE** time their journey to their Arctic breeding grounds to catch the wave of spring grass along their route so they can refuel on the way.

FINDING THE WAY

Flying animals are not only the greatest travellers on Earth, they are also the greatest navigators. They can find their way across continents and oceans, to and from places they have never been before.

WHOOPING CRANE
(Grus americana)

MONARCH BUTTERFLY
(Danaus plexippus)

South-west!

An internal clock and large eyes allow **MONARCH BUTTERFLIES** to monitor the sun's position at all times and work out which way is south-west, so they can keep flying in the right direction.

Learning from mum and dad

WHOOPING CRANES migrate from northern Canada to Texas. Young birds make their first trip with their parents, following landmarks like mountains and rivers. They learn more each year and get better at navigating until they too can guide their own young.

Mind map

CUCKOOS lay their eggs in the nests of other birds. Young cuckoos must migrate from Europe to Africa without their parents' guidance. Scientists think they have an instinctive sense of which direction to fly in and for how long, like an inbuilt map.

COMMON PIGEON
(Columba livia)

COMMON CUCKOO
(Cuculus canorus)

Flying for home

PIGEONS use the sun's position, an inbuilt clock, and the Earth's magnetic field to tell them how far north or south they are from home. Closer to home, familiar scents, sounds and landmarks guide them over the last few miles.

Follow the stars

Many songbirds migrate at night and use the pattern of the constellations to work out which way to go.

REDWING
(Turdus iliacus)

INDIGO BUNTING
(Passerina cyanea)

Ride the wind

WANDERING GLIDER DRAGONFLIES travel from India to Africa every autumn but they choose to ride the wind rather than navigate! They travel high up at 1,000m, where winds blow steadily from India to Africa. When the wind changes in spring it carries them back.

WANDERING GLIDER DRAGONFLY
(Pantala flavescens)

Smell trails

Seabirds in the tubenose family have a powerful sense of smell. **ALBATROSS** home in on the smell released by plant plankton as it's eaten by krill to help them find food. **MANX SHEARWATERS** use the smells of ocean currents, winds and familiar land to fly thousands of miles back to their nests.

MANX SHEARWATER
(Puffinus puffinus)

SHORT-TAILED ALBATROSS
(Phoebastria albatrus)

HOMES UP HIGH

Even flying animals that spend months in the air must come in to land when they want to have babies. Flight allows them to build their homes out of reach of predators to keep their young safe.

BAYA WEAVER BIRD
(Ploceus philippinus)

CAVE SWIFTLET
(Collocalia linchi)

Dangling domes

BAYA WEAVER BIRDS build nests of woven grass, dangling over water. The entrance tube points downwards, making it extra difficult for predators to steal eggs or chicks.

Spit nests

Birds called CAVE SWIFTLETS nest high on the walls and roofs of deep caves. They make nests from sticky spit that hardens in the air and glues the nest cup to the rock.

HOODED MERGANSER
(Lophodytes cucullatus)

Hanging around

Bats flip as they come in to land, to hang upside down from their hooked toes. Up to 20 million MEXICAN FREE-TAILED BATS roost in the roof of Braken Cave in Texas. Tiny HONDURAN WHITE BATS hang under leaf tents that they make by biting large rainforest leaves.

WOOD DUCK
(Aix sponsa)

HONDURAN WHITE BAT
(Ectophylla alba)

MEXICAN FREE-TAILED BAT
(Tadarida brasiliensis)

Up! Up! Down! Down!

Some ducks, such as MERGANSERS and WOOD DUCKS, fly up to nest in tree holes. When their babies hatch they can't fly down to reach water, so they just have to jump and hope for a soft landing!

Paper on a stalk

WASPS chew wood into pulp to build nests of hollow hexagonal cells where the queen lays her eggs. The nest hangs from a narrow stalk, so eggs and grubs are kept safe.

NORTHERN GANNET
(Morus bassanus)

COMMON WASP
(Vespula vulgaris)

Seabird cities

Seabirds can reach remote islands and sheer cliffs where they can nest more safely, close to the sea.

Around 39,000 pairs of **GANNETS** nest on Grassholm Island off the Welsh coast.

GUILLEMOT eggs have a pointed shape which makes them roll in a circle, rather than off the edge of the cliff.

Urban high rise

PEREGRINE FALCONS nest on high cliffs. Tall buildings such as church spires and apartment blocks work just as well and have brought peregrines into the heart of many cities.

COMMON GUILLEMOT
(Uria aalge)

PEREGRINE FALCON
(Falco peregrinus)

FLIGHT, FLOWERS AND FOREST

More than three quarters of all plants depend on flying animals to pollinate them and to scatter their seeds. These relationships between plants and animals are essential for habitats to thrive.

Colours and shapes

Flowers evolved in order to attract insect pollinators, so without insects there would be no flowers.

Bowl-shaped flowers such as **BUTTERCUPS** reflect light and warmth and are easy for many kinds of insects to land on.

The lip of **PEA FLOWERS** is a landing pad for **BEES**. When the bee reaches in to get nectar, its back is dusted with pollen.

DAISY FLOWERS have a ring of many tiny flowers at their centre containing nectar to attract small insects.

BUTTERCUP

WESTERN HONEY BEE (Apis mellifera)

PEA FLOWER

WHITE-TAILED BUMBLEBEE (Bombus lucorum)

DAISY FLOWER

ANGELICA and other open, flat flowers are good for **BUTTERFLIES**, **HOVERFLIES** and small **BEETLES** to land on.

LONG HOVERFLY (Sphaerophoria scripta)

ANGELICA

Tube-shaped flowers like **AUBRETIA** need the long tongues of **BUTTERFLIES** and **HUMMINGBIRDS** to reach the nectar inside.

PEACOCK BUTTERFLY (Aglais io)

AUBRETIA

Long-haul delivery

In tropical forests, the distance between two plants of the same species might be too great for insects to cover. Here some plants are pollinated by **BATS** and **HUMMINGBIRDS** who can fly further.

DURIAN BLOSSOM

SMALL FLYING FOX
(Pteropus hypomelanus)

GLITTERING-THROATED EMERALD HUMMINGBIRD
(Chionomesa fimbriata)

Colour coded

Plants colour-code their flowers to attract the pollinators they want.

At night there's not enough light to see colours, so **BAT**-pollinated flowers are white to stand out in the gloom.

BIRDS' eyes are great at seeing red against green leaves, so **HUMMINGBIRD**-pollinated flowers are red.

BROMELIAD

UV COLOURING

BEES don't see red well but they can see ultraviolet, so some flowers scatter UV light to create a glowing halo, clear to insect eyes.

DARWIN'S ORCHID

Closer and closer

Sometimes flowers and pollinators evolve together, and over time develop more and more specialised relationships.

THYNNINE WASP
(Zaspilothynnus trilobatus)

HAMMER ORCHIDS make a scent so like the smell of a female **THYNNINE WASP** that males try to mate with the flower and get a pod of pollen stuck to their backs.

DARWIN'S ORCHID has nectar at the end of a tube up to 43cm long which can only be reached by the long tongue of a **MORGAN'S SPHINX MOTH**.

HAMMER ORCHID

MORGAN'S SPHINX MOTH
(Xanthopan morganii)

TROUBLE IN THE AIR

Flying animals can travel over a wide area to search for food. Combined with an ability to breed fast and form huge flocks or swarms, this can spell trouble. For many insects and some birds, human crops, forests and even bodies are just dinner.

Delivering diseases

Flying insects that feed on human blood or human and animal faeces can spread disease-carrying microbes. Worldwide around 700,000 people die each year from diseases spread in this way.

Malaria and mozzies

In tropical countries the microbes that cause malaria live in the bodies of some **MOSQUITOES**. Female mosquitoes need a meal of blood to be able to lay eggs, and when they feed on humans their needle-like mouths inject the malaria microbes into the blood.

MOSQUITO
(Anopheles funestus)

Too tempting

A field of newly planted seed, tender leaves or ripe grain or fruit is too good to resist for flocks of birds such as **PIGEONS**, **CROWS** or **GEESE**. Modern bird-scarers play recordings of alarm calls to scare them away and protect crops.

CARRION CROW
(Corvus corone)

Parrot vandals

KEAS are large, clever parrots from the mountains of New Zealand. They learned to perch on sheep and peck the fat from their backs. Farmers shot thousands of them, and now keas mostly use their mischievous skills on campers, ripping open tents and damaging cars!

KEA
(Nestor notabilis)

Forest plague

In America, the grubs of **MOUNTAIN PINE BEETLES** have destroyed millions of pine trees by eating the inner bark. Warmer winters due to climate change allow more beetles to survive until spring.

MOUNTAIN PINE BEETLE
(Dendroctonus ponderosae)

Flying famine

LOCUSTS form vast swarms which can cover areas up to one and a half times bigger than New York City, and are able to eat almost 200,000 tonnes of plants each day. They can fly hundreds of miles in a day and eat fields of crops in minutes. Farmers from Mexico, Africa, India and China fear locust swarms.

DESERT LOCUST
(Schistocerca gregaria)

RED-BILLED QUELEA
(Quelea quelea)

Most numerous bird on Earth

RED-BILLED QUELEA from Africa can fly long distances and breed fast to make the most of the continent's scattered rainfall. Flocks millions strong gather to make the most of human crops too.

Heroes in Flight

Humans have depended on the abilities of flying animals for thousands of years. Despite all our modern technology, there are some vital jobs that animals still do best.

Pigeon post

PIGEONS' homing skills make them perfect message carriers. Homing pigeons were used by the ancient Greeks and Genghis Khan, and in both World Wars pigeons were taken in tanks onto the battlefield and released to fly back to headquarters with messages.

HOMING PIGEON
(Columba livia domestica)

GOSHAWK
(Accipiter gentilis)

Hunting with eagles

'Falconry' – the practice of using trained birds of prey for hunting – could be even older than pigeon post. Falcons were used to catch small mammals for food and sport, but eagles and eagle-owls could bring down larger animals. Today **GOLDEN EAGLES** are still used to hunt wolves in Khazakstan and Uzbekistan.

GREATER HONEYGUIDE
(Indicator indicator)

Talking with a bird

When a Yao hunter in East Africa wants to find honey, he calls a **HONEYGUIDE**! The little brown bird understands the call, replies, and leads the way to a bees' nest. The hunter breaks into the nest to get the honey and the bird is rewarded with a feast of bee grubs and wax.

AGAVE

MEXICAN LONG-TONGUED BAT
(Choeronycteris mexicana)

BUFF-TAILED BUMBLEBEE
(Bombus terrestris)

TOMATO

COMMON BLUE-BANDED BEE
(Amegilla cingulata)

COCOA

TREFOIL HORSESHOE BAT
(Rhinolophus trifoliatus)

COFFEE

ALMOND

WESTERN HONEY BEE
(Apis mellifera)

Crop connections

A third of all human crop plants rely on insects, birds or bats to pollinate them.

Many tropical plants including fruits like avocados and mangoes and desert plants such as agave are pollinated by **BATS**.

Farmers growing tomatoes in greenhouses keep **BUMBLEBEES** in little cardboard homes to pollinate the tomato flowers.

Coffee is pollinated by **HONEY BEES** and many kinds of **WILD BEES** and **BUTTERFLIES**.

Cocoa is pollinated by tiny **FLIES** and perhaps the **BATS** that come to feed on them.

Oranges, lemons, apples, pears and almonds all need **BEES** to pollinate their flowers so fruits and nuts can grow.

Only bees make honey

It takes the nectar from two million flowers, gathered by **BEES** while flying over distances of around 90,000km, to make one jar of honey!

WINGS UNDER THREAT

Bird, bat and insect numbers have fallen drastically around the world and many species are in danger of extinction. Habitat loss, pollution, insecticides and climate change are some of the challenges they face. But there are things that we can do to help.

SOUTHERN HAWKER DRAGONFLY
(Aeshna cyanea)

Flower power

Park keepers and gardeners can plant wildflower meadows, but even a window box can provide nectar for bees and other insects.

Be messy

Let your garden get a bit messy. Nettles, wildflowers and other 'weeds' provide food for caterpillars, and dead plants provide good shelter for many insects. And never, ever use insecticides!

Wet and wild

Big wetlands are important for many insects, bats and birds. But a garden pond, even one as small as a washing-up bowl, can be a haven for flying wildlife.

WHIRLIGIG BEETLE
(Gyrinus substriatus)

HOUSE SPARROW
(Passer domesticus)

GRAY BAT
(Myotis grisescens)

LAYSAN ALBATROSS
(Phoebastria immutabilis)

Leave bats in peace!

Human disturbance of bat caves can stop them breeding and hibernating. In the US, humans even introduced a deadly disease called white-nose syndrome. Protecting caves allows bat numbers to recover.

No plastic, please!

Many seabirds can't tell the difference between bits of plastic and proper food. LAYSAN ALBATROSS scoop it up by accident and feed their chicks with it, sometimes killing them. You can help by making sure you use less plastic and never let it get in the sea.

Climate crisis

Climate change is messing up the pattern of the seasons, making it hard for animals to breed, hibernate or migrate at the right time. This is especially difficult for flying animals that migrate long distances, who can no longer rely on good conditions for their journey or the right weather at their destination.

EUROPEAN BEE-EATER
(Merops apiaster)

BARN SWALLOW
(Hirundo rustica)

Climate action

We can all help to fight climate change. Use your bike or your feet instead of a vehicle, put on a jumper instead of turning up the heating, eat less meat and, perhaps most important of all, tell everyone you know how important it is to take up the fight for our planet!

MYTHICAL WINGS

Before the invention of hot-air balloons and aeroplanes, flight seemed like something beyond human ability. In many cultures the sky was thought to be the home of the gods, so it's not surprising that flying animals seemed powerful and full of magical abilities. Almost every culture across the world has myths and legends about creatures that fly.

Changed to a bird

Birds have often been thought to carry the souls of the dead. In ancient Mexico, the native Aztec people believed that fallen warriors became **HUMMINGBIRDS**.

Atlantic sailors believed **SHEARWATERS** held the souls of drowned sea men.

MANX SHEARWATER (*Puffinus puffinus*)

LONG-TAILED SABREWING HUMMINGBIRD (*Pampa excellens*)

Winged gods

The ancient Egyptian god Horus was shown as a man with the head of a **FALCON**.

The Hindu deity Garuda had both human features and the wings of an **EAGLE**.

Some Native American cultures believed in the thunderbird, who ruled the sky and was carved at the top of totem poles.

HORUS

GARUDA

THUNDERBIRD

Special messengers

In Celtic myths both **RAVENS** and **BEES** were thought to be able to carry messages between humans and the other world of gods and the dead.

Good and bad luck

BATS are often associated with darkness and evil in Europe and America, but in China flocks of bats are the bringers of good luck and plenty, and they are used to decorate household objects and clothing.

Bird people

For the Maori people of New Zealand kites are very important.

They are thought to allow humans to communicate with the sky god Ranginui. Kite flying is an important part of all new year celebrations.

Precious feathers

Feathers were essential to Aztec life as they were used to decorate headdresses and clothes for ceremonies and everyday life. Aztec cities were full of aviaries with captive birds of all kinds, kept to provide the millions of feathers used every year.

GLOSSARY

CAMOUFLAGE

This is when an animal matches its environment in order to stay hidden from predators or to sneak up on prey.

CLIMATE CHANGE

For centuries, humans have used fossil fuels such as coal, oil and gas to power cars and factories and generate electricity. This has increased the amount of carbon dioxide and other so-called 'greenhouse gases' in the atmosphere. This traps more heat at the Earth's surface, changing weather patterns around the world and melting icecaps, leading to rising sea levels.

DISPLAY

A display is something that an animal does to communicate with another member of its own or another species. Peacocks spreading their tails and humpback whales singing are examples of a display

ECHOLOCATION

The ability of bats, dolphins and a few birds to make sounds, listen to their echoes and create a picture-in-sound of the world around them. Echolocation allows these animals to find their way around in the dark of night and the deep ocean.

EVOLUTION

Evolution is the process by which living things change over time, developing into new forms shaped by the need to survive in different conditions. For example, a fish with slightly bigger fins can glide for a moment and escape being eaten. Its small-finned companions are eaten instead, and only it survives to have babies which will inherit its big fins.

EXOSKELETON

Insects, such as butterflies and beetles, and crustaceans, such as crabs and shrimps, do not have bones inside their bodies. Instead they are protected by a hard, armour-like outer layer called an exoskeleton.

EXTINCTION

When all the members of a species have died out, so that no young can ever exist again, that species is said to be extinct. Many species are becoming extinct because of the way humans are treating our planet.

FOSSIL

A fossil is the remains of an animal or plant, preserved in stone. The rocks in which they are found tell scientists how old fossils are, so they can give us a record of how life on Earth has changed over millions of years.

GLOSSARY

HABITAT

The place where a plant or animal lives. Habitat refers not only to the landscape and climate of an area, but also to all the other plants and animals which live there. The plants and animals in a habitat are connected to each other so that they can only thrive as a community. Habitats are also connected to each other, making a network of life that encircles the whole Earth and of which we are a part.

INVERTEBRATE

Invertebrates don't have a backbone or internal skeleton, but many of them, such as insects and crustaceans, have a tough exoskeleton that gives their bodies shape and protects their insides from damage and drying out.

LARVA/LARVAE

A larva is the baby stage of an animal that is very different from the adult. Caterpillars are the larvae of moths and butterflies, and tadpoles are the larvae of frogs and toads.

MIGRATE

Animals which move from one location to another in a seasonal pattern are said to migrate. For example, European swallows migrate from Africa to Europe in the spring and back again in the autumn.

MISSING LINK

During the process of evolution, living things change gradually over time and many generations, so that entirely new groups of living things are formed. Species like Archaeopteryx, which have the characteristics of their ancestors and their descendants, show how one group is linked to another and are often called missing links.

NECTAR

The sweet, sugary liquid that flowers make to tempt insects, birds and bats to visit them, so that the flower can dust them with pollen to carry to another flower.

PARASITE

A plant or animal which uses the body of another living thing as a place to live. A host is the animal on which the parasite lives. The host may be severely damaged by the parasite, or hardly notice it.

POLLEN

Pollen is the dust-like material made by flowers and carried to other flowers by the wind or by animals. Just as a sperm fertilises an egg so it can grow into an animal, pollen fertilises ovules so they can become seeds and grow into new plants.

GLOSSARY

POLLINATION
In pollination, the male parts of a plant, called 'anthers', make dusty pollen that travels to the female parts, called 'stigma', to fertilise its seeds. Most plants rely on animals to pollinate them, and almost all habitats on land depend on these pollination relationships.

PREDATOR
An animal that lives by hunting, killing and eating other animals. The animals it eats are known as prey.

SPECIES
A kind of living thing. Each species of animal, plant or fungus has features which help it to survive and make it different from every other species. For example, one bird species may have a hooked beak and strong talons for hunting, while another may have webbed feet and a rounded beak for swimming and eating water plants. Living things can usually only breed with other members of their species.

RINGING

Birds' legs and bats' wings can carry tiny metal or plastic rings with a unique number. When the bird or bat is recaptured or if it dies and its ring is found, it can help to build a picture of where the bird has been.

TAGGING

Electronic tags that record position and beam it to a satellite are now small enough to be put on creatures as tiny as a mouse, so their movements can be tracked exactly.

VERTEBRATE

Mammals, birds, reptiles, amphibians and fish are all 'vertebrates', meaning they have a spine or backbone, which is part of their internal bony skeleton. This supports and protects the soft parts of their body, giving them shape and helping them to move.

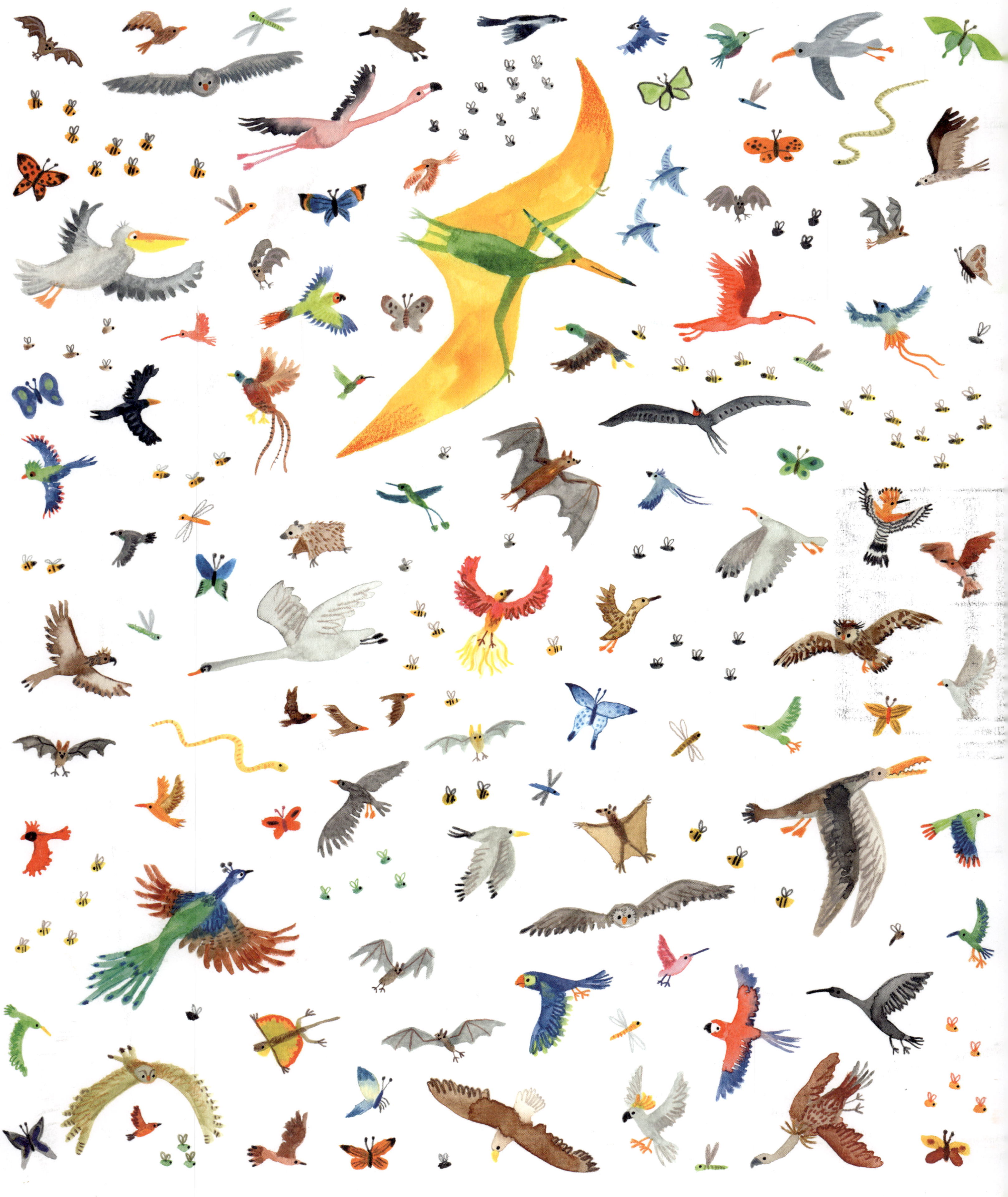